HONEYCOMB

M. R. Peacocke

HAPPENSTANCE

ACKNOWLEDGMENTS:

Some of these poems, or earlier versions, have appeared previously in collections from Peterloo Poets or Shoestring Press. Seven new poems are published here for the first time.

Previous collections from M. R. Peacocke:

- *Finding the Planes*, Shoestring Press, 2015
- *Caliban Dancing*, Shoestring Press, 2013
- *In Praise of Aunts*, Peterloo Poets, 2011
- *Speaking of the Dead*, Peterloo Poets, 2003
- *Selves*, Peterloo Poets, 1995
- *Marginal Land*, Peterloo Poets, 1988

Printed by The Dolphin Press
www.dolphinpress.co.uk

First published in 2018 by HappenStance Press,
21 Hatton Green, Glenrothes, Fife KY7 4SD
nell@happenstancepress.com
www.happenstancepress.com

CONTENTS

for
Stella Barnes

EASTHAM STREET

Afternoon. The chip shop is closing.
Opening hour now for terrace doors.
Wedges of shadow hold ajar
the terracotta, flaking brown,
ginger and glossy beige.
Hopscotch pavements gleam.

This is the old women's time.
Belayed on cords of fraying breath
they rock on broad shoes to the top of the street
to settle on benches, screaming
like harbour gulls. *Forgot yer pinny, Doris!*
One wears a comfortable hat.

Lightly the northwest wind brooms aside
trash of clouds and words.
Propped on a taffrail of houses,
the old women cruise till tea
on salt unvisited blues and greens
of the distant bay.

THE BUS

A stiff climb, the three steps. He opens a brown fist
and counts out the right fare. Five rows back most often,
the shady side today. Shady side today, aye. A'right, Ted?
A'right, aye. Tweed sleeve sits by tweed sleeve most Saturdays;
today one lean brown arm settles alongside another.

The bus eases away, chirruping and groaning, heaving
at bends. The lane turns; below them a chequered valley
shines, familiar as a kitchen, and there is nothing
to be said of it, they know it like a mother. Their talk
is all of vegetables, the trenching and ridging,

hoeing and forking. Purple-top it's too warm, split at the core.
Peas gone dry and the spinach bolting. Taties I can't
just tell. Corn, though, corn and tomatoes. Marrows, aye.
Come October give the Lord his due with a good mixed basket
at the altar steps and a monster blue cabbage.

Special prize at the Show that ought to get. Aye.

Eloquence is fading now. A few more weeks until the time
of caps, oiling of tools, storing away, and winter to be endured
like a sleepless night. Past the big estate, roundabout,
Ford garage. Hospital the next stop. Now then, Ted.

PRACTICE

She haunts me with a bridled patience,
and when she comes, as now she's come,
my heart keeps stumbling, can't perform
as it agrees it should; but *Nonsense,*
Darling, she cries—she is crying—clinches
of irritation in her throat, and shame
obstructing mine—*It simply needs more time,*
more time and work, until it's effortless!
But in her smile and in her spine
there's effort, as in her turn of phrase.
Her ash is in my hair. My god,
can't she accept how it is to be dead?
While I still blame her, she can know no peace,
her yearning and critical heart being mine.

AFTERNOON

The wool rolls down. The needles droop.
A spider at the corner pane
schemes for a pittance line by line.
The dull doves in the neighbouring wood
call *Could you do   Do do   You could.*
A wakeless lull that's less than sleep
brims in her eyes and palms and lap.
Something is finished. Nothing's done.
A lapse, a loss, a truce, a peace.
One lacewing trembles at the netted glass.

ON THE WAY DOWN

An old ewe kesent[1] among rushes, lodged
belly up in her blanket of dirty fleece,
cleft stare fixed on dying.

Our fists clenched deep into ragged wool
couldn't haul her up to rights. Only her fear
buckled her back to life

and sent her lurching from the smell of us
and the alien voices, out of our hands,
till at last she settled

to the sweet rummage of grass. Months, perhaps;
maybe a spring to nourish a spindling lamb.
So we took on the fleece

of doubtful weather, looking back at times,
and followed the harsh track down. One more season?
We are making old bones.

---

1 *kesent (adj.)* : Cumbrian dialect: (sheep) stuck on its back.

HONEYCOMB

How nimble the old are, balancing
as the world gyrates beneath them—fast—faster.
All that's familiar sweeps from touch
till their bones are honeycomb.

You can't know how deftly I'm spinning
or how I love anything that hesitates—pauses—
sticks with me a minute—touches
my flying head. Look,

I've gathered a little parchment leaf.
It settled against my cheek as damp and cool
as a child's kiss. We have happened
together. We slip away.

RUNNING

Once there was running, a spurt of joy
in the feet, some unbidden riot
under the skin. Then there was running,
willed. Now the body's dull as lips
of animals mumbling frozen grass,
and if I say, *Do you remember running?*
it pauses, puzzled. It knows its tasks.
It can't recall.

SKIN NARRATIVES

Body transcribes itself monkishly
over seven years, each edition
less well bound, the scribal errors
grosser, blanched code of scars
a faulty braille still legible
even in palimpsest
on the thin vellum of hands, shins, wrists,
record of accident and skirmish:

a tin I was trying to open
that opened me (the kitchen cupboard
leant and delivered a hard clout);
Aunt Jessie's favourite glass
shivered into arrows, sheaved there
in my bare foot; a neat
pearl-handled pocket-knife turned spiteful—
these stitch marks in my palm to prove it—

the bright, bulging cabochon of blood
amazed me. This zigzag? That's the streak
of white in my mother's brown hair.
She's on her knees, picking
gravel out of mine, and I bite
silently on raw jolts
of pain because Grandma's in mourning
for her scarlet begonias, smashed.

PUT

At last my door, and putting everything down
to fumble for the key before life to come

and becoming aware of Put: these bags, weight
of potatoes, a couple of jars, all the stuff

settling into a sideways loll, and there it is,
put: burdened but neutral, awaiting guidance,

and I'm tasting the powerlessness of the object
(though there was, once, a fear that the dead might rise)

when oh, there goes the milkman's horse, my childhood's
loved horse-mountain, moving without command but clop

by clop and stopping gate by gate, the dead stoop
of gravity in the lift and plant of his vast

and simple hooves. No decision, but inherent
in each put, the atlastness of arriving.

THESE HANDS

These hands have been dangling beside me
all along, links of padded bone,
though I've scarcely noticed: the first folds,
creases, indentations, written
into palms and digits well before
I barged two-fisted into air,
nervous finger-ends securely backed
with a slip of the same chitin
as rhinoceros horn, kestrel claw,
ladybird carapace, crab shell.

Masters of the dumbshow, guiding me
beyond seven ages, comforters,
thieves, warm as fleece, accusers, icy,
blind dancers in the rites of flesh,
sufferers, scratchers: now they are old
I blame them for stumbling about,
poor labourers, curling on their pain;
yet when I come to stretch my spine
in rough indifferent ground, they'll lie there
patiently beside me, like dogs.

ALLOTMENT

On the allotments, few of us about.
Saturday is match day. Random sounds
drift over, scrap-paper idle.
From blackmost tips of limes not yet
in leaf, the rooks keep comment.
Thin shouts from distant swings.

Through a hole in the hedge, cat
carries his silence; pauses; scratches up;
squats, with a hard yellow stare.
The blackbirds fall silent.
This happens, that happens, mostly
nothing happens, but the peas are planted

and a row of shallots to tamp the season in.
Then take a shortcut home by way
of a mesh of shadow
where headstones lean, one to another,
quiet. Work is done, and no more need
now, to do anything: just stand.

LATE

An end. Or a beginning.
Snow had fallen again and covered
the old dredge and blackened mush
with a gleaming pelt, but high up there
in the sycamore top, *Thaw,*
Thaw, the rooks cried,
sentinel by ruined nests.

Water was slacking into runnels
from drifts and pitted snowbacks,
dripping from the gutter and ragged
icicle fringes. Snow paused
in the shining embrace of bushes
waiting in ledged curds and bluffs
to tumble into soft explosions.

And suddenly your absence
drove home its imperatives like frost,
and I ran to the high field
clumsily as a pregnant woman
to tread our names in blemished
brilliant drifts; because the time we have
is shrinking away like snow.

LUNAR

Moon doesn't read much, is her own volume
slightly foxed, her own stained page. She's up there
leaning becalmed in a lunar dawdle
(doesn't she know it's morning already?)
but I was up last night as well, watched her
racing round, handed cloud to cloud, ice-hot.
We are old, tarnished, half-erased, absurd
and, when we think there's no one looking, dance.

WINTER FESTIVAL

The lights are awake in streamers and posies.
Time now to gather in the maiden aunties,
the grandmothers, settle their posture brightly
where they cannot fall, bless them with sweet sherry,
anoint their faces with well-seasoned music
and let the fires burn let the fires burn. Now stack
all the empty days into a little pile,
put a match to them, watch them flame and shrivel.

When all have eaten a slice of winter pie
it's time to fold them away fold them away
as before, follow the comfortable creases.
Happy soon, dears, happy when, happy painless.
Our rituals all are ended, the doggerel
tapped through for the year and the halting gospel
of the cold spelled out in words almost unknown
to the children, who will nod and say amen.
                    Bye, Aunty. Bye, Granny. Amen.

CLINIC

Knees withstanding.
Feet sometimes at nod
with unshaped words.

Hands in couples,
each palm a parent
to the other.

Don't be anxious.
This is my body
bequeathed to me.

Each stillbound head
laden with its world,
solitary.

SUNDAY DIARY

Vicar came, soft hands and smiling.
A little talk with God amen
and then there was Songs of Praise.

Lovehate the rightness righteousness
of hymn tunes, how the harmonies
move in step like nuns, supportive
maintenance of the melody
(like women's underwear, modest
but assured and feeling, we hope,
nice.) The holy paths of the tunes
are for those among us younger
or unsure of holding a part.
Sometimes there's the very top-floor
extravagance of a descant
above the secure foundations
but then in due course down we go,
safe and sound, cadence descending
with the no-nonsense of a lift
achieving ground level. How sweet
the thought of Sunday closing, bells,
church wardens, choirboys, and good news
of a wedding with proper banns—
and yet my spirit won't stay still,
keeps up its butterfly shuffle
unreconciled against the pane,
its dusty lisp, craving the light,
the wild cold air that will kill it.

HULK

Rusting encumbered hulk, you may sink when you like,
zigzag downward, founder. I want to be shot of you.
With one deft shudder, if I could I'd grow permeable,
translucent, flex through barnacled plates and strakes,
skinny-dip upwards, flow into enormous light;
but the cramped submariner heart, so long labouring
below decks, is deaf with habit, turns its back on me,
tinkers among its dirty oils and won't give in.

TAKING LEAVE

When she was leaving
(taxi at the door, engine running)
he wrote, beyond speech,
the familiar hand grown sketchy,
I didn't know you were going so soon.

And it's like that, people leave,
sooner than they thought,
sooner than they knew, and things
don't wait, and a lifetime
isn't enough to recover the words,
uncover, discover the words.

WHAT THE BIRD SAID

Flick of shadow, chip of song.
A robin came, glancing,
turned the puff of himself
towards me, rosehip or copperleaf
according to light;
opened his beak on a winter breath,
shook out tremors of music.

A loss, a death, was stuck
hard as a gall in my throat.
I was foolish for consolation,
wanting a god to be angry with.
Shadows. December sun.
Oak apples, twigs, dry leaves. A bird.
Nothing but this, it said.

SHALL WE DANCE?

Dew almost frost. It's the heeltap
of summer, October's pourriture,
and drunken bumble bees are plunged
head down in buddleia nectar, stuck
to the narrow goblets, trembling,
or tumbled to the yellow
of aftermath, helpless, signalling
prayers with a hooky leg.
What shall we do about the mess?

A few small flies still reel
among the diagonals of light,
where leaves leak like inverted plops
of air from goldmouth fishes,
and there isn't a bird whose voice
is not derelict. Time to strike
a lucky match among the trash
and watch how sap still forces
bubbles out of a chopped branch.